D0207736

THE STORY
OF A WONDER MAN

BEING THE AUTOBIOGRAPHY

OF

RING LARDNER

THE STORY
OF A WONDER MAN

BEING THE AUTOBIOGRAPHY

OF

RING LARDNER

ILLUSTRATED BY MARGARET FREEMAN

GREENWOOD PRESS, PUBLISHERS
WESTPORT, CONNECTICUT

Library of Congress Cataloging in Publication Data

Lardner, Ring Wilmer, 1885-1933.
    The story of a wonder man.

    Reprint of the 1927 ed. published by Scribner, New
York.
    1. Lardner, Ring Wilmer, 1885-1933--Biography.
I. Title.
PS3523.A7Z52 1975   818'.5'209 [B]   75-26216
ISBN 0-8371-8414-2

This edition originally published in 1927 by Charles Scribner's
Sons, New York

Reprinted with the permission of Charles Scribner's Sons

Reprinted in 1975 by Greenwood Press,
a division of Williamhouse-Regency Inc.

Library of Congress Catalog Card Number 75-26216

ISBN 0-8371-8414-2

Printed in the United States of America

Foreword

By Sarah E. Spooldripper

THE publication of this autobiography is entirely without the late Master's sanction. He wrote it as a pastime and burnt up each chapter as soon as it was written; the salvaging was accomplished by ghouls who haunted the Lardners' ash bbl. during my whole tenure of office as night nurse to their dromedary.

Some of the copy was so badly charred as to be illegible. The ghouls took the liberty of filling in these hiatuses with "stuff" of their own, which can be readily distinguished from the Master's as it is not nearly as good. Readers and critics are therefore asked to bear in mind that those portions of the book which they find entertaining are the work of the Master himself; those which bore them or sound forced are interpolations by milksops.

Another request which I know the Master

would have wished me to make is that neither reader nor critic read the book through at one sitting (Cries of "Fat chance!" and "Hold 'em, Stanford!"). It was written a chapter at a time and should be perused the same way with, say, a rest of from seven weeks to two months between chapters. It might even be advisable to read one chapter and then take the book back to the exchange desk, saying you had made a mistake.

Mr. Lardner's friends will regret that he omitted from these memoirs reference to his encounter with Mussolini, the Tiger of France and Italy. The two happened to be occupying the same compartment on "The Dixie Flyer" between Cannes and Mentone.

"Great golf weather," remarked the Tiger.

"I beg your pardon," replied the writer. "Je ne parle pas le Wop."

I forget what else happened.

Contents

CONTENTS

Illustrations

[ix]

ILLUSTRATIONS

[x]

. . . I hurried home to exhume diaries and notes.

Introduction

BY the employment of methods amounting almost to the so-called third degree, the
heads of the publishers syndicate who I am
under contract has finally got me to write
my autobiography, a task which I shrink
from it like Pola from a camera, yet which
the doing of which I feel I owe it to my
public.

This then is the first installment, but will
precede same with a brief acct. of the comical scene in the publishing offices which
culminated in me undertaking to do the

work under certain conditions. In the first place I was decoyed into the offices by a letter from the boss saying they was a package waiting there for me from a admire in Yuma that looked like salt water taffy. This was a hoax and I hadn't no sooner than entered the door when I was bashed in the stomach by some blunt instrument, probably a wardrobe trunk. When I regained conscious I was laying on my back in the gun room while the head of a midiron had been shoved into my mouth with the heel resting vs. the roof of same and the toe on the tongue, and a Mr. Perkins the manager had began to pull my teeth with some blunt instrument. When this had got past the amusing stage I told them I would do what they wanted provided the work was not published prior to my death.

"That suits us," said the boss, "if you'll promise to die by the Fourth of July."

The others took up the refrain:

"If you'll promise to die
By the Fourth of July."

Agreements were then signed and I hurried home to exhume diaries and notes containing the material necessary for a accurate autobiography and will now begin writing it with a determination to stick to facts and to not let the truth be interfered with by a personal modesty never excelled and perhaps only equalled in this generation by well, maybe Oscar Wilde and Belasco.

. . . "Little Ring, au naturel, was bathed in pure
alcohol . . ."

Chapter 1

The Birth of a Wonder Man

THE first week in March, 1885, was a gala
week throughout the civilized world, the
United States in general and the latter's
great middle west in particular. In this one
week there was an unfounded rumor of a
royal betrothal between Queen Victoria and
King Gillette; a young Washington dentist,
Dr. Ghoul, watched a mixed fivesome tee

off at Chevy Chase and predicted that four of them would have pyorrhea; the Lardners of Niles, Mich., announced the birth of a fourteen pound man child, and almost on the same date twenty-nine years later, or maybe it was 28th of June, the Archduke Ferdinand was shot down at Serajevo.

These events occurred before there were telephones or telegraphs and the news of the Lardner boy's birth had to be flashed to the world by runners. Sparing no expense, the parents hired Paavo Nurmi to notify distant relatives and engaged Charlie Paddock for the sprints. In less than two weeks the Niles post office began to be flooded with letters of all kinds, most of them being circulars from strangers advocating the installation of an oil heater. "They pay for themselves in what you save on coal," was the general gist. But there were also more personal letters of which I will take the liberty of printing one from Clarence Mackay:

"Don't write. Telegraph! Flowers telegraphed to all parts of the world."

And one from a travel service company:

[5]

"I understand that your little boy is contemplating a trip to Egypt and I am writing to ask if you will not help me to secure his booking and plan an independent trip for him, if that is what he wants. I supply you with steamship tickets, issue travelers' checks, letters of credit and baggage insurance, etc."

And one from a hotel training school in Washington, saying:

"There is a nation-wide demand for trained men and women in hotels, clubs, restaurants, cafeterias."

Also came a request from Edward Bok for the baby's autograph and a letter from Ray Long, asking for first chance at any short stories the newcomer might write. Excitement ran high and even to this day the first week in March is set aside in Niles as "Have a Baby Week."

As a result of careful living and a strict adherence to the doctor's orders, the child was able to take his first meal at table early in June. Both the haute and demimonde of Niles were asked in and when the dishes had been cleared away, a bath tub was set in the middle of the room and little Ring, au naturel, was bathed in pure alcohol, the guests afterwards dipping pipes into the tub and blowing soap bubbles. This was in the days before they had horses and boats and when you wanted to go from one town to another, you had to take a train.

Chapter 2

The Boy Grew Older

THIS autobiography started out to follow the style of Edward Bok and Henry (Peaches) Adams and refer to the hero in the third person, but the idea has been abandoned because in my case it would be confusing on account of two of my interminable brothers also being named Ring (inspiring a Niles wag, Charles Quimby, to call our family the Three Ring Circus) and if I were to write that Ring did this or Ring said that, the reader would not know whether I meant myself or one of the other boys unless in each instance I gave the full designation, a practice that would eat up too much space. For my oldest brother was christened Ring Once For Ice Water; another one, Ring Twice For Towels, and I, Ring Three Times For Good Luck. So from now on the author will be spoken of as I, provided it ain't too hard to locate that unaccustomed key on my typewriter.

As all we boys began being born one after

another it became necessary to take drasti-
cal action in regards to the intra-mural traffic problem. For example there was so many
mouths to feed that only a third of same
could be accommodated in the dining room

Those that had their meal was trying to get out and those
that was still hungry was trying to get in.

at one time and the confusion and congestion
was something fierce when those that had
had their meal was trying to get out and
those that was still hungry trying to get in.

A new door was cut into the wall to be
used for eat-bound traffic only and my sis-

ters took a course in barking and served as traffic cops, but the situation would of soon gotten intolerable only for nine of the boys suddenly deciding to leave home. Five went to Leavenworth, two to Atlanta and two to San Quentin. The roving spirit proved contagious and soon a tenth, Gregory, entered Yale and won his Y as coxcomb on the varsity crew. Still another, Polycarp, obtained employment as a Chicago caddy. A Chicago caddy is a boy who carries your ordnance bag, retrieves sliced or hooked bullets and replaces divots in bystanders.

None of we children was ever allowed to talk at table, but as soon as a meal was over we were encouraged to talk as much as we liked and in that way I got quite a reputation as an after dinner speaker. This was in my third year, 1888, when Taylor and Presser were running for President and Vice President against Polk and Beans. The Taylors lived right across the street from us, but it was a different family. The Taylor who was elected President was Zachary Taylor, while the Taylor near us was H. N. Taylor, the feed man. No relation to the other Taylor.

H. N. Taylor had a daughter, Livid Taylor, who suffered from contusions by a prior marriage. Livid was my first sweetheart, which she will learn for the first time if she reads this. I was too young (only three) to know the exact wording of a formal declaration and so kept my love a secret, but many is the night I cried myself to sleep in regards to Livid Taylor and her contusions.

In March, 1891, a few days before my sixth birthday, the postman brought an invitation, for our whole family, to attend the Inaugural Ball. In those days the event was held not in Washington, but in Seattle, to make it more exclusive, as it was figured that very few congressmen and foreign diplomats would have the money to go way out there, or the inclination either, the train running only as far as Duluth and from that point you had the choice of walking or creeping on all fours. Those who chose the former method of locomotion usually relieved the tedium of the journey by rolling a hoop.

The invitations were always purposely sent out so late that only people who lived right near Seattle could hope to get there in time, and they were not invited. You may imagine that our home was a scene of bustling activity from the instant the card reached us till it was time to board the train for Duluth. I was taken along because there was no one to leave me with, and to help open the car windows.

We left Niles at noon on the third day of March and did not reach Duluth till the morning of the sixth. This was before the era of patent couplers and the cars of a train were fastened to one another with gay ribbons. (It was in 1895 that the Santa Fe adopted hooks and eyes.) The result was that every mile or so, the engineer would feel a lightening of the pull on his "iron horse" and would find on investigating that two or more cars or even the entire train had been left far behind, in fact four hours after the "start" of the trip it was discovered that the engine was way up in Wisconsin while the train was still standing in the station at Chicago with the conductor hoarse from shouting "What's the matter?"

Everybody felt kind of blue when we arrived in Duluth at last and realized that we were already thirty-six hours late for the ball and with at least three weeks separating us from Seattle. Some were in favor of returning at once to Niles, but wiser counsel prevailed and we prepared to complete the trip in the hope that the difference in time between Minnesota and the Coast would work to our advantage.

Chapter 3

Young Man Goes West

THE trip from Duluth to Seattle was rather uneventful and can be dismissed in a few well rounded paragraphs. In those days, as I pointed out in the preceding chapter, no trains ran west of Minnesota and neither boats nor horses had been invented. It was believed that the only possible way to cover the mileage between the new Scandinavia and the Pacific Coast was afoot or on all fours. But a few moments before we were about to set out by one of the last named methods, my Uncle Walrus learned from the telephone girl at the hotel, a Miss Scurvy, that other travelers had successfully negotiated the distance on sleds drawn by teams of dogs and we decided that nothing could be lost by trying this innovation, for if it proved a flop (an expression of my grandfather's) we could still get off and walk or crawl.

So many of the other guests had been

tipped off to the sled gag that all but one of
the dogs in Duluth were already chartered
by that time, so we had no choice but to
engage the remaining one, which turned out,
to his mother's surprise, to be a four months
old Sealyham. We hitched him up to two
sleds, the front one for our party and the
trailer for suit-cases, mess kits, golf bags,
etc. We were insured against thirst by Uncle
Walrus, who in playing thirty-six holes of
golf during our stay in Duluth, had luckily
acquired a handful of water blisters.

It was a gay crowd for the first two hundred miles. My sister Ann, an accomplished
musician though otherwise an oaf, played
chords on the dulcimer to such songs as
"Promise Me," "Killarney" and "What'll I
Do?" and my fresh young voice made the
welcome ring and the Ring welcome all
through the Dakotas. We stopped for the
night at Bismarck, where my little brother
Croup insisted on fishing for herring. Luck
was with us and we didn't have a bite,
though the Sealyham kept scratching himself.

Next morning the latter began to complain of glanders, brought on, he said, by
working like a horse, and it was a relief to
him and the rest of us when Uncle Walrus
and Aunt Chloe and their two children died
of exposure and had to be pushed off the
sled. With the load thus lightened, we made
Butte the second night and registered at
the Montana-Biltmore, where Jack Bow-
man was then head bell beagle. News got
out that I was in the city and the fire whistle
blew from eleven o'clock till ten minutes
after. We learned in the morning that it was
just a grass fire.

"It was just a grass fire," Jack told
us.

On Saturday night, March 9, we arrived
in Seattle and found with joy that, through
a stroke of good fortune, the ball was still
in progress. It seems that Young Stribling
was dancing with Dolly Madison, had been
dancing with her, in fact, since the night of
the fourth, and they couldn't end the ball
because they couldn't make him let go.

I was recognized by Texas Guinan, led to

the middle of the floor and introduced to Mrs. Madison.

"And," said the latter, "I want you to

Mrs. Madison was free and I whirled her away.

shake hands with my partner, whom I have nicknamed the Georgia Clinging Vine."

Without thinking, Stribling loosened his hold with his right arm to shake hands with me and Miss Guinan at the same time grabbed his left and jerked it away. Mrs. Madison was free and I whirled her away to

THE STORY OF A WONDER MAN

the strains of "Nervous Breakdown." Paul Whiteman* was leading the orchestra.

"Well, Mrs. Madison," I said, "you look kind of peaked. You look like you was suffering from the grip."

"Anybody that battles with Young Stribling suffers from the grip," was the reply of Old Hickory's madam.†

Before the second encore, I was calling my partner "Dolly" and she was calling me "Lard" and that night marked the beginning of a friendship that soon ripened into apathy.

Seattle in 1891! In the morning, tram rides to the French market; at noon, luncheon in Limehouse; five o'clock tea in the

* Editor's note: This must be a mistake. In 1891, Paul Whiteman was only a year old.

Author's note: It was a different Paul Whiteman.

Editor's note: Must have been.

Author's note: Was.

† Editor's note: Presumably another mistake. James Madison was known as "Sunny Jim," never as "Old Hickory."

Author's note: Your father died of electricity.

Presidio; at night, baseball results, dinner music and the Dickens Hour.*

The day after the Inaugural Ball, my family started back east, leaving me at the hotel in lieu of a check. My next seven years, between my sixth and thirteenth birthdays, were spent up and down the Pacific Coast and I would not trade the experiences of that period for a passport picture of Bull Montana.

* Editor's note: The last eight words seem to refer to radio. Radio was unheard of in 1891.

Author's note: You're an old fool.

A squirrel-tender's job was to keep the squirrels out of the trees
so the people would have some place to sit.

Chapter 4

Bright College Years

ALONE in Seattle at the age of six, broke, and indebted to the hotel in the amount of $26.50 for board and room. How many kids would have faced a situation like this with equanimity! But I never lost confidence that I would find a way out. I forget just now what I did do; suffice it to say that inside of seven years I was in San Francisco, playing a cornet, evenings, at Tait's on the beach, and in the daytime working in the park as a squirrel-tender. In those days there were no benches in the parks and a squirrel-tender's job was to keep the squirrels out of the trees so the people would have some place to sit. Inasmuch as there were 186 squirrels in this particular park and I had only one assistant, you may imagine that I was kept hustling; squirrels get mighty tired of staying on the ground and would employ every imaginable subterfuge in their efforts to climb the tempting trees with which the park was plentifully supplied. Outwitting them and keeping them on terra firma developed both my brains and speed and ten years later, when my three runs of the length of the field won Yale a championship game, 4 to 2, an Associated Press commentator said "Harvard was beaten in the parks of San Francisco."

In the fall of this year an S. O. S. was broadcast from Chicago—that gargantuan metropolis was in flames as a result of a cow named O'Leary dropping a lighted cigarette in a roll of films.*

Every city of importance sent a volunteer fire company to the rescue. The company organized in San Francisco was composed of myself and Bill Lange, later to become famous as a ball player and dancing instructor. This, of course, was before horses or camels were thought of and Bill and I had to drag our hose cart east afoot. Bill was very little help and by the time we reached our destination, the fire was out and I was sixteen years of age.

It was now time to think of college. Stories of my all-around athletic prowess had appeared in all the papers and I received tempting offers from virtually every university of standing. I thought first of entering the Harvard Law School.†

* Editor's note: This must be a mistake. Mr. Lardner is writing about the year 1898; the Chicago fire occurred in 1871.

Author's note: There is a considerable difference of time between Chicago and San Francisco.

† Editor's note: It would have been impossible

Finally I decided to divide up my first year to the best advantage, going in the fall to Michigan, which needed a half back with a sextuple threat, spending the winter at Amherst, where a high class basketball guard was wanted, and winding up in the spring at Tulane, which was anxious to land a good pitcher who could also pole vault, hurdle, throw the javelin and run as anchor man in the relay. With a schedule thus outlined I had leisure to write and enjoy myself in a social way during the summer months.*

It was now that the Spanish war broke out and I enlisted as a general.

for Mr. Lardner at his age and with his credits, or lack of credits, to enter the Harvard Law School.

Author's note: That's why I thought of it first.

* Editor's note: Mr. Lardner, asked to explain the meaning of sextuple threat as applied to a half back, said it meant a half back who could not only kick, pass and run forwards, but also run backwards, act as field judge and announce the results of out-of-town games. He said that in all football history there had been only four really great sextuple threaters—himself, Marilyn Miller and the Mayo Brothers.

Chapter 5

How Spanish War Ended

THE chief difficulty about the Spanish war lay in finding out where it was being held. The censorship was so strict that even we who had enlisted as generals were kept in the dark as to the location of hostilities and there was some talk of mutiny unless the government came across and at least confided in us whether to march our divisions north, south, east or west.

It was all right to have some civilian come up to you and say "How is the war, General?" because then you could reply, "Fine, thank you," but when they asked you "Where is it?" that was a horse with another collar. We all had to have two sets of uniforms, white for home and gray for traveling, because there was no telling if the battles were to take place at our park or on the road.

While we were still in this chaotic state,

three big pieces of news reached Chicago on successive days—one that Grant had taken Vicksburg, the second that Admiral Farragut had vanquished the Spanish fleet in Manila Bay, and the third that General Miles

There was some talk of mutiny.

had surrendered to Lee Shubert at Appomattox. The war was over and there was such a divergence among the opinions of the fight experts that no historian has a right to say who win.

Excursion trains were now run from all points in the United States to Washington to accommodate the applicants for pensions. I will never forget my first ride on a sleeping car. In those days it was against the law to have berths run the length of the train; they had to be cross-wise, and inasmuch as it was necessary for them to occupy the entire width of the car and also, on account of the uppers, extend from the floor to within a couple of inches from the roof, why you can see that both passengers and crew had their troubles when there was occasion to walk from end to end of one car or from one car to another.

As a rule, passengers gave it up entirely and from the time the berths were made up till they were taken down, why the best bet was to stay right in your berth; that is provided you were there when it was made up; otherwise there was no way for anybody but Houdini or a veritable sliver of a man to get to bed. The railroads offered huge wages for conductors, trainmen and porters measuring so little in circumference that they could make progress through the infinitesimal crack between the top of the uppers and the top of the cars and after dark it became customary for the members of the crew to strip themselves and grease their entire carcasses to facilitate fore and aft intra-mural travel.

It was owing to these conditions that I made the acquaintance of Professor Ashley Snoot. Prof. Snoot had Lower 6, and I was supposed to be right above him in Upper 6.

"Prof. Snoot," I said, "how do you pronounce your name?"

"Through the nose," replied the pedagogue, calling long distance. "But I thought you would want to talk to me about biology, as I am Professor of Biology at the University of Chicago."*

"All right, Prof.," I said. "What do you think of biology?"

"It's a wonderful idea," replied Prof.

* Editor's note: Prof. Snoot was never connected with the University of Chicago.

Author's note: That is the telephone company's fault. The number is Midway 100.

Operator's note: The number has been changed to Midway 2,000.

Author's note: Well, let's have that number, please.

Snoot, "but can they enforce it? We have had it now since January 1920, and they tell me there is more drunkenness than ever; why, I understand that women, who never drank before, are now insisting on a cocktail before dinner."

"Where do they get it, Prof. Snoot?" I inquired.

"Call Main 2461," said the Prof.

We were now entering the station at Washington. In those days all trains stopped in the White House garage and it was up to me to get cleaned up for my presentation to President Hayes.

Chapter 6

How I Threw Big Party for Jane Austen

IT was at a petting party in the White House that I first met Jane Austen. The beautiful little Englishwoman had come to our shores in response to an attractive offer from the Metro-Goldwyn-Mayer people, one of whose officers had spelled out her novel "Pride and Prejudice" and considered it good material for a seven reel comedy. Syd Chaplin was at that time with this firm and was slated for the title rôle.

Miss Austen had a few weeks' time to spare before she was due in Hollywood and it fell to my lot to entertain her. I postponed my engagement with President Pierce, whom I intended to interview in regard to my pension as general in the Spanish war, and placed myself entirely at the disposal of the little authoress. She expressed a desire to see the night life of New York and

I organized a party to visit Texas Guinan's. In the party, besides myself and Miss Austen, or Janey as we called her, were Brinck Thorne, then captain of the Yale football nine, and Harry Wills.*

After two or three rounds of drinks we decided we had had enough and a waiter brought us a check for $22.75. The other two men seemed to have paralysis of the arms and as I found only $1.50 in my pocket, I asked Miss Guinan if she would take my check. She said yes and I made out a check on the Great Neck Trust Company, but knowing my balance there was only $7.00, I purposely neglected to affix my signature. Miss Guinan's sharp eyes noticed the oversight and asked for my autograph. This piqued Miss Austen as she was really more famous than I at that time, so to smooth matters over I suggested that we all give

Editor's note: The author evidently means "eleven," not "nine."

Author's note: Other teams would not play against Mr. Thorne unless he limited himself to eight helpers instead of the regulation ten.

Miss Guinan our autographs and start an album for her.

I next took Miss Austen to Albany to meet Gov. Al ("Peaches") Smith. The governor received us with his usual simplicity

She expressed a desire to see the night life of New York and I organized a party to visit Texas Guinan's.

and said he was a great admirer of Miss Austen's work.

"I thought 'The Green Hat' was a scream," he complimented her.

Miss Austen wanted to go to Hollywood by way of Pittsburgh, but at that time there was a federal law forbidding any railroad to run a train near that city. President Pierce was a born hater of Pittsburgh and remained in that frame of mind to his dying day. "Janey" was obliged to make the journey via Niagara Falls. She eventually reached Hollywood and supervised the screening of "Pride and Prejudice," which made a big success under its new title, "The Bath in Champagne."

It was about a month subsequent to my affair with Jane that the world was startled by Robert Fulton's invention of the taxicab. The first taxi now would seem a crude vehicle, but at the time it was hailed as a marvel. It was a sidewheeler and was steered from the rear seat, by the passenger, thus insuring at least, its arrival at the point where the passenger wanted to go. The driver sat in front and warned pedestrians out of the way. He generally did this by cupping his hands to his mouth and shouting, almost continuously, "Halloa! Halloa!" For a while the new conveyances were known as "Halloa cabs."*

* Editor's note: They still are in some cities.

Facsimile of a letter to the author from Jane Austen.

The strain on the driver's voices was so great that very few of them were able to hold their jobs after a week or two. There was danger of the whole thing falling through because of the dearth of leather-lunged shouters and to obviate this, Fulton invented a musical instrument called the slide trombone and drivers were taught to play Berlin's "All Alone," the inference being that the cab wanted the street to itself. The instrument was so constructed that in case the pedestrians did not take warning from the melody, the driver could push the slide to its extreme length and knock them out of the way.

Fulton's achievements made him so popular in New York that he was given the keys to the city of Boston and a one way ticket to San Diego. It is estimated that the earnings of his taxicabs had run well over fifty dollars when they were suddenly cut off by the invention of the horse.

Horses were very uncertain at first. For example, you would bet on one that was a favorite at some such price as 3 to 5 and seemed to have far and away the best chance to win and along would come an 8 to 1 shot and make your horse look like a sucker.*

I recall once visiting the Saratoga race-course in the administration of President Fillmore and meeting a man named Bud Fisher, a portrait painter and fancier of horse flesh. He had just paid $12.00 or $12,000, I forget which, for a horse named Hyperion, had engaged a star jockey, Earl Sande, to ride him and advised me and other acquaintances to bet on him. We followed the advice, and the horse ran a very good race, but the jockey was left at the post, sitting in the middle of the track. It was quite laughable.

* Editor's note: "Sucker" was a slang invention of the author's, meaning probably in this case, "dub" or "flop."

Chapter 7

New York's Noon Life

THE furore over the invention of horses by Thomas A. Edison had no sooner abated than the country was thrown into a new ferment of grape juice by John F. ("Peaches") Hylan's discovery of the subway. People who now ride in subways in various cities and complain of strap-hanging, overcrowding, etc., would scarcely believe the facts concerning that first New York subway, or tuber as it was called on account of its resemblance to a potato. Instead of being obliged to pay a nickel apiece for a ride, passengers were sent engraved invitations and the number of same was limited to the seating, or rather, lying down, capacity of the trains; say forty or fifty individuals who expected to be particularly busy at their office on Monday received subway cards for that day; forty or fifty others, whose busy day was Tuesday, were invited to ride that day, and so on through the week.

Each car was equipped with half a dozen four poster beds, half a dozen twin beds, three or four easy chairs and a chaise lounge. Later the twin beds were taken out of the equipment because so few twins seemed to be in business in New York; more correctly, many sets of twins were in business, but not in the same line and not particularly busy on the same day. For example, the Kitchell twins, Howell and Growell; they both had offices downtown, but Howell was a fishmonger with an exclusive Friday trade, while Growell sold welts and by tacit agreement, out-of-town welt buyers visited New York Mondays only. And it was the same with other sets of twins.*

These early subway cars had straps, stout leather straps, but they were not fastened

---

* Editor's note: These facts are brought out in other autobiographies of the early nineties.

Author's note: What of it?

to the roofs of the cars. They were loose and were used either for sharpening razors or for amusement purposes. Passengers used to play a game called "Have You Heard This One?" Each passenger was required to tell a story and if any of the other passengers had heard it before, the raconteur was given a hiding with the straps. This was where Growell Kitchell picked up most of his welts.

It was during the early days of the subway that Emile Zola visited New York and remarked in broken French: "Why, you New Yorkers are like ze little animals, what you call them, ze moles. You are always burrowing in ze ground." Horace Greeley was much taken with this comment and made a suggestion that was afterwards put into effect—that the city be divided into burrows, the Burrow of Brooklyn, the Burrow of the Bronx, etc.*

At this time Lily Langtry was the toast

* Editor's note: The Oakland Mole in San Francisco Bay got its name in much the same way.

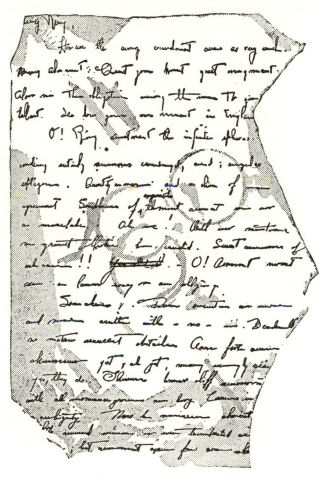

Facsimile of a letter to the author from Lily Langtry.

of New York. Co-starred with the Marx Brothers in "A Texas Steer," she swept Broadway and was next given a job sweeping the cross streets. Mayor Walker presented her with the keys to St. Louis, but she refused to take the hint and it became my duty to show her around Gotham.*

Unlike Jane Austen, who had insisted on visiting the night clubs, Lily wanted to see the city's noon life. Nothing gave her more of a thrill than to lunch at one of the sidewalk tables outside the Pennsylvania station and watch the zinc-workers and hatters at their midday revels.

"Vive!" she would shout as some particularly daring peasant girl tossed a ringer or a leaner, or an extra hilarious traffic policeman successfully coaxed a perambulator in front of a taxi or Halloa cab as they were then called.

"But listen, Lil," I often remonstrated, "don't you want to even get an impression of what goes on in places like the Knicker-

* Editor's note: A pseudonym for New York.

bocker Club or the Lambs or Sophie Tucker's or places like that?"

"No, Lardy," she would reply.*

So a party of four or five of us, usually consisting of H. L. Mencken, the Marx Brothers, Ward and Vokes, Barnum and Bailey, the Duncan Sisters, the Striblings, the Bison City Quartette, the Happiness Boys and the Four Horsemen, besides myself and the Langtry, would daily engage a corner table at Seventh Avenue and Thirty-third street and, as I have said, enjoy the antics of the tradesmen out for their noon lark.

At length Mayor Walker asked me to take Lil to Atlantic City as she had never seen an auction sale. But it happened that just at this period a law had been passed against auctions, said to be the only law ever passed in New Jersey. So all that the Langtry and I could find to do was walk up and down, walk up and down. I noticed that she grew more and more uninterested and one day she

* Editor's note: She called him Lardy.

yawned several times and then uttered an exclamation of tedium.

"No wonder," she said, "they call this the Bored Walk."

So all the Langtry and I could find to do was walk up and down, walk up and down.

Chapter 8

Football Trick Uncorked

ALL this happened in the summer of my seventeenth year and in the fall I made up my mind to go to college. As told in a previous chapter, I had decided to start in at the University of Michigan, but at the last moment I received a better offer from Yale and the first day of September found me in Lancaster, where Yale was then located, ready to take my entrance examinations.

Entrance requirements at that time were a great deal more exacting than at the present day. One had to pass with a grade of fifty in at least three major studies. I selected spelling, arithmetic, and English literature. I can still recall the five words we were asked to spell, namely Scott Fitzgerald, Zelda Fitzgerald, Scotty Fitzgerald (their daughter), Rube Goldberg (one of their friends), and St. Paul (where Mr. Fitzgerald came from). I spelled two and a half of the words right, giving me the required mark of fifty.

The arithmetic test consisted of two questions, the first of which was, If four sailors go into a corner grocery and buy three cakes of soap at five cents a cake, what is it? The answer was tar soap. The other question was, Give the telephone numbers, residence and business, of five successful stevedores. In this test I scored one hundred, or as the examiners called it, a sweep.

In English literature we were required to name the criminal in the three following stories from "The Adventures of Sherlock Holmes"—"The Speckled Band," "The Engineer's Thumb," and "The Copper Beeches." I got the first two all right, but by the time I came to the third, the gin which was then passed around between every two questions, began to make me sleepy and I wrote down "Never mind." However, I had won low medal score and the next thing on the programme was football.

I shall never forget the first day I reported for football practice. Now, at New Haven, they have a field so big that they call it the Bowl. Our field at Lancaster was so small that they called it the Ash Tray. The Yale team was then being coached by John Paul Jones, a grandfather of Tad Jones. Ted Coy was the captain, but there was a rule that if, on the first day of practice, any candidate appeared who was more beautiful than the captain, he supplanted the last named. Thus it was that I captained Yale in my freshman year.

I will omit the details of the first week's practice, which embraced the usual fundamentals, such as pumping up the ball, mending holes in the bladder, lacing and unlacing, and throwing your hat over the cross bar of the goal. We were scheduled to play Harvard the first Saturday, as it was then figured, and correctly, that if the hardest game came first, there was much less of a strain on the players through the balance of the season. In fact, as soon as the Harvard game was over, the squad used to let up gradually week by week until by the time of the final game of the season, usually with Maine or Harrisburg High School, the majority of the athletes were so stewed that they came to the field in their pajamas or went to the wrong field entirely.

On the Friday before the Harvard game, I overcame my natural diffidence and began to inspire the men with such expressions as "Come on, men!" "Keep at them, men!" etc., and when one of our players made a particularly good stroke, I never failed to say "Bravo!" or, if it was a girl, "Brava!"

All the chairs were taken half an hour before the big game started. There must have been a hundred and twelve people in the Ash Tray. First the Harvard partisans would give their cry—"Mind over matter, men! Mind over matter!"—and from across the Tray the Yalensians would shout back: "Fight for Old Eli and Root for Elihu, Root!" The rival bands played their battle hymns, Harvard's melodious "Break the News to Mother" vying with the Yale classic, "Ridi, Pagliacci." The two teams, each shy one man, who was drunk, tiptoed on the field so as not to let the crowd know they were there, and thus avoid the danger of rioting.

I hardly tried in the first half and we failed to score. Harvard was also held scoreless. In our dressing room, between the halves, Coach Jones lit into some of the men mercilessly, telling them their faults. "Heffelfinger," he shouted at a big guard, "you didn't clean your nails this morning. As for you, Coy, you quit tickling Thorne in the back of the neck from now on." And so forth. He criticised everybody but me.

Most of the second half went by and still there was no score. The crowd had gone home stiff.*

Finally the field judge stopped the game to find out what time it was. He was a painter and could not work after four-thirty. The players' watches all disagreed and the official ruled that it was four

* Editor's note: The author probably means "bored stiff."

Author's note: The h—ll I do!

twenty-nine, which was what his cousin, Charley Brickley's, watch said. With a minute to play, I uncorked the trick I had

"Heffelfinger . . . you didn't clean your nails this morning."

been holding in reserve all through the game. I neglected to mention that two days prior to the battle, we had sent Harvard a set of our signals and they, knowing every play as it was called, were able to stop it.

But now I called a signal that was not in the set we had sent them. It was for Jim Braden to deflate the ball, pack it up and send it back to the manufacturers with a complaint that it was defective. The mail box was back of Harvard's goal line and the Harvard team stood aside and allowed him to make the touchdown, never suspecting that the ball was in that neatly wrapped bundle. That is the true story of my first big victory over Harvard, 5 to 1.

Chapter 9

Yale, Beaten by Blind Boys

AFTER the Harvard game I tendered my resignation as Yale captain because my incumbency was making some of the men so miserable. Every night when they were put to bed, Thorne and Coy and Butterworth cried with such plaintiveness that none of the other athletes could sleep. Coach Jones frequently walked the floor with them all night; he even gave them an extra bottle at bedtime, but to no avail. However, the rest of the squad would not stand for my retirement and the problem was ultimately solved by our trading the three malcontents to Dartmouth for a practice ball.

With the team thus strengthened we went on and won the Trinity and Villa Nova games and reached the big annual Thanksgiving Day battle against Miss Spence's

School with a record of three victories and
four defeats, having been nosed out on successive Saturdays by Moler's Barber College, the War College of Washington, La
Salle Extension University and the Weehawken School for the Blind.

I might say in passing that the last named
institution beat us by trickery. When we
came on the field, our opponents were
sitting at various corners with their eyes
closed and tin cups in their hands in which
passers by were expected to drop coins. I
was taken in and would surely have dropped
a dime in the opposing captain's cup had it
not been a habit of mine never to carry
more money in a game than was necessary
to tip the officials. Some of the other boys
loosened up, however, and as soon as the
cups were filled, the "blind" men opened
their eyes with a whoop and proceeded to
give us a licking. At that we might have
trimmed them if, the night before the game,
we hadn't gone out and got blind ourselves
to make it more even. The Weehawken
team's college color was light yellow and

this was the origin of the expression blind man's buff.*

With the approach of Christmas I was swamped with invitations from classmates

Mrs. Grudge was social dictator of New York and Staten Island.

to spend the Holidays at their homes. I accepted the invitation of Jack Grudge, son of Henry Grudge, then president of U. S.

* Editor's note: The above paragraph is followed in the manuscript by a description of the game between Yale and Spence. It is vulgar.

Author's note: So is your old man.

Steel. Grudge père's fortune was estimated
in the hundreds and Mrs. Grudge was social dictator of New York and Staten Island; no one could claim to have "made"

Her father rented a covey of tigers and had them there in
the house.

Society until he had been in the Grudges'
palatial town house at West Sixteenth
street and the river.*

There were two daughters in the family,
Vera and Bera Grudge, co-eds at Princeton.
Vera was a pretty, interesting girl, but Bera,

* Editor's note: This house is now occupied by
the Cunards.

besides always wearing rompers, was what the French would euphemistically call nutté. To whatever remark you addressed to her, she would reply "Sis-Boom-Ah! Tiger!" Her father rented a covey of tigers from the Bronx Zoo and had them there in the house, hoping she would get disgusted with them, but she would lie right down in front of them, look them in the eye and sis-boom them ad Nassaum. Her father said to me one night:

"Lardy," he said, "I'd give anything to get Bera married off."

"All you have to do," I replied, "is get her married. She is already off."

"The trouble is," he continued, when the laughter had died down to a certain extent, "that she is tiger mad. She won't look at a human."

"Well," I said, "about your only chance is to marry her to a blind tiger."

Jack Grudge afterwards told me that his father certainly enjoyed my visit.

The Grudges had so many house guests that Christmas that it was necessary to institute a first and second table system for meals. I sat at the second table between Bera and the laundress, a Mrs. Stevens. Our banter would often be interrupted by Bera just when Lydia (Mrs. Stevens) and I were "going good."

"Mrs. Stevens," I would say, "I once had a sister who was quite fond of one of her gowns, but she would wear it only in the front yard."

"Why?" This from Mrs. Stevens.

"She said it was her laundress."

"Sis-boom-ah! Tiger!" This from Bera.

On another occasion Mrs. Stevens told me that another guest, a Mr. Spurl, brought his laundry down to her and bet her she couldn't "do it up" in four hours.

"Did he win?" I inquired.

"He lost his shirt," said Mrs. Stevens (Lydia).

"Sis-boom-ah! Tiger!" This from Bera.

At five o'clock the next morning the four of us set out on a dog-sled.

Chapter 10

A Gay Christmas Eve

CHRISTMAS EVE at the Grudges'! No Christmas Eve since has seemed like anything at all. With all their wealth and position, my host and hostess and their children were intensely democratic and their servants joined in the festivities on an equal footing with the family and guests. In fact, Mrs. Stevens (Lydia), the laundress who sat beside me at meals, was quite the life of the party and kept us in spasms of laughter. For example—

"Mr. Lardner," she said to me as we watched Bera Grudge and the hostler trim the tree, "I suppose I may expect a present from you."

"Yes," I replied, "and it will be something appropriate for a person of your calling. I am going to give you a cuff in the neck."

"If you do," she retorted without an instant's hesitation, "I will be hot under the collar."

"Underwear, did you say?" I put in.

"Sis-boom-ah! Tiger!" murmured Bera.

This was before the invention of evergreens and the baubles and candles were hung on a shoe tree.

When the tree had been trimmed, the question arose as to who would hang up the stockings.

"Why not Mrs. Stevens?" I said jokingly. "She certainly ought to be an expert."

"I'll hang one on your jaw in a minute," teased the laundress.

A few moments later, Mr. Grudge, whom his friends called Doc because his home overhung the river, suggested:

"Let's have some carols."

"But don't bring Earl!" said the laundress.

The singing was interrupted by the noise of an infant's cries upstairs.

"Is that your baby?" I asked Mrs. Stevens.

"Yes, sir," she replied, and Gus Kahn and Walter Donaldson,* who were at the party, got their idea for a song hit from those two simple lines.

As we were all separating for the night, Mrs. Grudge asked me whether I would care to accompany her and Vera and Bera on a mission of charity early Christmas morning.

"Every Christmas," said Mrs. Grudge, "the two girls and I visit some worthy poor family and try to take the curse off what would otherwise be for them a dismal day."

I assured her I would be delighted, so at

* Editor's note: Kahn and Donaldson claim they were not there.

Author's note: Were too!

five o'clock next morning, the four of us set out on a dog sled (This was before the days of surf boards) and drove to the home of an Italian family named Chianti who lived in penury.*

There were fourteen Chianti children, so Mrs. Grudge kissed their father and then handed him an odd-shaped bundle.

"I've brought you a bird," she said, "and I wish you a merry Christmas."

Afterwards, on the sled, she asked me what kind of bird I thought she had given him.

"Well," I said, "I suppose a family of that nationality would prefer a guinea hen."

"Nevertheless," said Mrs. Grudge, "what I gave him was a gull. He will open the bundle thinking it is a turkey or something else edible, and when he sees what it is, he will tell his kiddies the joke and the laughter will be general all day."

"Last year," spoke up Vera, "mother pulled an even better one than that. She

* Editor's note: A suburb of Brooklyn.

[59]

gave a great big package to a starving family by the name of Weaf, saying 'Here is a goose for you,' and there was nothing in the package but a picture of Goose Goslin of the Washington ball club."

"Sis-boom-ah!" commented Bera.

When we got back to the Grudge home, there were three horses in the living room, Doc's gift to his two daughters and son Jack.

"Oh, father!" shrieked Jack. "Just think! Three of them!"

"A horse apiece," remarked Mrs. Stevens, peeping in from the laundry.

It was now time to examine the stockings. In mine I found an orange, a flashlight, a mechanical toy (A Negro that did the Charleston), a box of crayons, some candy and a miniature chess set.

"Oh, Mrs. Stevens," I cried excitedly, "see what I found in my stocking!"

"And see what I found in mine," she replied.

I looked. It was a run.

Chapter 11

How I Swam the Hudson

THE Holidays were over and it was time to go back to Yale, then located, as I have said in a previous chapter, at Lancaster, Pa. The first hazard was the Hudson River, which was quite difficult to cross in those days of no boats. I asked a handsome, big traffic policeman how to set about it.

"Take the Desbrosses Street ferry," he advised.

At Desbrosses Street and the River, however, I learned that no ferries were running because no boats of any kind had yet been invented. I found out afterwards that the traffic policeman was none other than A. D. Lasker, famous two years later as the designer and builder of the first boat. At the time he spoke to me, he was doubtless so full of his dream of boats that he thought they were already actually in existence.

On the corner of Hudson and Spring

Streets, I asked directions of a friendly looking vendor of shoe laces.*

He told me to walk way up past Troy on the East bank of the river, and look for a Ford. After what seemed to me a rather tedious stroll, I passed through Troy and began looking all over for a Ford, but couldn't find one—or any other kind for that matter. I told my troubles to a farmer, who laughed heartily and said:

"Mon, mon! (He was a Scotchman) Ye are long before ze day of ze automobile. When your New York friend said 'Ford,' he meant 'a place in a river where it may be crossed by wading.'"

Embarrassed and chagrinned, I walked down to the river bank and removed my shoes, stockings and plasters, as this seemed as narrow and shoal a point as any other.

"What's the idea?". inquired a deep voice which I discovered belonged to a

* Editor's note: This was undoubtedly Mary Lewis.

Author's note: No. It was a man.

Editor's note: My mistake.

white-bearded old fisherman who was dredging for chocolate covered almonds.

When I told him my plan, he tried hard to discourage me.

"You will never make it. No Yale man ever has, and only five Princetonians."

"What Princeton can do, so can Yale!" I replied, and sang two stanzas of the Yale song—"Beulah, Beulah!"

Covering myself from head to foot with grease, I stepped boldly into the treacherous stream, which at that juncture is twenty-eight feet wide and knee deep. In less than half a day, I was on the west bank, but wish to state that I owe my success quite as much to the encouragement given me by Whiteman's orchestra, which accompanied me in a tug, continuously playing "Rocked in the Cradle of the Deep," and "Abide With Me," as to my fine physique and mastery of the crawl stroke.*

Unable to break off the habit all at once,

* Editor's note: Mr. Lardner was the first to employ the crawl stroke, covering the entire twenty-eight feet on his hands and knees.

I crawled down to Albany and caught the night boat back to New York.*

From New York, I crossed to Jersey by ferry and decided to enter Princeton, as it

Whiteman's orchestra accompanied me on a tug.

was closer and I had heard there were vacancies there on the hockey team and the mandolin eleven. Also I was attracted by the promise of an occasional glimpse of my late host's daughters, Vera and Bera Grudge, co-eds at Old Nassau.

Our hockey season began inauspiciously.

* Editor's note: Boats had, by this time, been invented.

In the first place, the athletic association had neglected to provide a Puck and the local news-stands had sold out. On the opening night of practice, we played with a copy of Godey's Lady's Book, but it proved unwieldy. Moreover, it was an open winter in New Jersey and the lake was not frozen over.

"There is no ice," I said one evening to Bera Grudge, who had inquired how we were doing. "We ought to have some ice."

"Ring for a bellboy," was her view of the episode.

Perhaps I ought to explain, before proceeding, that hockey was not played quite the same in those days as it is now. The players numbered only two and their positions were, respectively, Go Way Back and Sit Down. The records will bear me out when I say that I was best Sit Down Princeton ever had, not even barring F. Scott Fitzgerald.

Our first big game that season was with Wesleyan and we lost it by default, both my teammate, Carson Hull (later known as Big Bill Edwards), and I forgetting all about it. Some of the undergraduates got very angry at us for this, and for many days, every time we would appear on the campus, they would point at us and shout: "You bad men, you!"

Big Bill broke it up the moment he stepped on the ice.

Chapter 12
I Transfer from Princeton to Medicine

AFTER the Wesleyan game fiasco, there was some talk of firing myself and Big Bill Edwards off the team and selecting other players to represent Princeton at hockey, but this idea was given up when it was found that we were the only two men in college who had skates.

Our second game was with my former alumna, Yale, and Big Bill, who was then known as Hull on account of his resemblance to that part of a ship, broke it up the moment he stepped on the ice. The balance of the hockey season was spent trying to get him out of the lake, where the fish were making vigorous complaints about the congestion. The lake was called Lake Carnegie after the library of that name, it being used as a receptacle for the students' books.

Owing to my success on the mandolin

club, where I played E string on one of the banjos, my name came to the ears of the Dean.

"Have you registered?" he asked.

I played E string on one of the banjos in the mandolin club.

"No," I replied.

"Well," said Dean Cornwell, "you register and we'll fix you up the best we can. But you can't have a bath because there is an Odd Fellows' convention here this week."

"What is his name?" I asked. "And why does he object to people's having baths?"

The Dean was greatly amused at my simplicity and in after years we met again and got a hearty laugh out of the episode.*

Dean Cornwell next inquired regarding my choice of a course.

"Well," I said, "six thousand yards is plenty if it's well trapped."

Once more I had displayed my naiveté and the Dean was in hysterics.

"Lardner," said he, "I wish you would stay at Princeton all your life. You are a yell!"†

Aided by the Dean's influence, I soon became a member of the Dekes, the Alpha Delts, the Phi Beta Kappas, the Kiwanis, and Realty Board and was rushed by the Triangle Club, the most exclusive of Princeton's social organizations. They rushed me

* Editor's note: *I* didn't.

† Editor's note: If Lardner had stayed there all his life, which he would have done if he had waited for his degree, he doubtless would have become known as the Princeton yell.

as far as Trenton and then relinquished the chase on my promise to enter the University of Illinois.

At Illinois I took up the study of medicine, a six months' course in those days, unless you were bright. Among my classmates were Harold (Red) Grange, L. M. (Mike) Tobin, C. C. (Chamber of Commerce) Pyle, and Fred (Peaches) Nymeyer. Illinois had the right idea about that bane of most medical students' existences—anatomy. It was the custom at that time for the instructors to employ some prominent undergraduate or alumnus and dissect him with a view to showing, for the pupils' benefit, his general structure and the location and function of his various organs.

Yale, for example, used Mr. Taft and it took two years to go all over him, even in a hurry. And the same at Michigan, where Germany Schulz was selected as the subject. At Illinois, on the other hand, we dissected one of Singer's Midgets and got through the course in one day, with an hour off for glee club rehearsal.

I was graduated in medicine and awarded my M. D. after only two months of study; moreover, I passed the final examination with a perfect mark of 100 and still have a copy of the questions and answers of that examination, which may be of interest to medical students and practicing physicians of the present day:

Q. Where is your appendix located? A. In Washington Park Hospital, Chicago, unless the cleaning woman has been in.

Q. How does the stomach act when you eat regularly? A. Surprised.

Q. What has been your hospital experience? A. Terrible.

Q. What would you do in a case of an epileptic fit? A. Call a doctor.

Q. What would you do if somebody had a stroke? A. See that they counted it.

Chapter 13

My Medical Career

MOST young doctors make the mistake of hanging out their shingles in large or small cities where there are already more medicos than can earn a comfortable living. At the time I received my degree, automobiles were just coming into vogue and after giving the subject considerable thought, I evolved the following scheme—to establish a gasoline station on a popular motor highway, far from any town; to run a restaurant in connection with it, and to keep secret˷the fact that I was an M. D. I selected a site halfway between Kansas City and Pittsburgh, put up two gasoline pumps and an attractive roadhouse and painted a sign, "Filling Station for Man and Motor." The sign itself amused everybody.*

For a wage of four dollars a week, I hired

* Editor's note: Not me.

a fifteen-year-old boy who, in infancy, had fallen through an open stopper in a wash basin and spent a week in the waste pipe, and ever since had had a horror of water in

He was so soiled and blurred that people began to languish the moment they saw him.

any form. By now he was so soiled and blurred that people began to languish the instant they saw him.

It was Roach's (this boy's) task to stand out in front by the gasoline pumps and as soon as customers stopped for gas, got a good look at him and started to droop, he would say, "Madam, or Sir (as the case might be), you ain't well. Fortunately, there is a doctor stopping with us," whereupon I would be summoned and would minister to my patient or patients, charging huge fees and getting away with it because Kansas City and Pittsburgh, the nearest points where another doctor might be reached, were so far distant. The only trouble with my plan was that my patients treated me as they would their own doctor and did not pay cash, but asked me to send them my bill, and invariably they gave me fictitious names and addresses. Occasionally, however, one of them paid for a meal and at the end of the first two months, my books showed a profit of $4.50, not counting the $20.00 which I owed Roach.

With this stake I moved to Chicago and rented a suite of offices at the corner of Madison and Paulina Streets, then the heart of the shooting belt. The suite comprised a reception room and a silo. There was no need of a consultation or operating room because by the time my patients reached the outer door, they were so full of stray bullets that it was too late to do anything but identify them. I made my money by keeping them in the silo until a reward was offered for information as to their whereabouts. Sometimes it was years or even never, owing to a way Chicago husbands and wives had in those days of leaving home on interminable bats, and as a rule, the party left behind either took the prolonged absences as a matter of course or was not aware of same.

The following incident is typical of the Chicago of that time:

A boy named "Hi" Fever was trying to acquire enough money to attend college by selling subscriptions to "Risky Stories." His father had suggested that he call on one L. H. Tweek. The boy rang the doorbell at the Tweeks' and Mrs. Tweek answered it. "Hi" asked if her husband was at home.

"I don't know," replied Mrs. Tweek. "I have a vague recollection that he said something about going to the 'Follies' opening at the Colonial."

"But," said the Fever boy, "that show's

opening was in December and it is now August."

"Is it?" exclaimed Mrs. Tweek. "Well, in another month we can have oysters again!"

My silo was finally filled to overflowing by unclaimed cases and it seemed advisable to move to another part of town. I put up a tent in Grant Park and hung out a shingle inscribed, "Surgeon. Cold Cuts a Specialty." The park was always popular with employees of Loop offices and department stores during their lunch hour and thousands of them took advantage of the opportunity to enjoy their midday meal and undergo some necessary operation at the same time. The potato salad which I served with the cold cuts was covered with a sort of ether dressing and from each patron I managed to remove at least his tonsils without his being any the wiser. A certified public accountant once estimated that if all the tonsils I cut out during lunch hours were laid end to end, it would be a nuisance.

I was now nineteen years of age and

thinking of getting married. I consulted a friend of mine, Dr. Flip.

"Dr. Flip," I said, "I was thinking about getting married."

"I wish I had," was his reply.

"What? Got married?"

"No," he said. "Just thought about it."

The chief lifeguard sat on the beach watching the drowners
drown and trying to figure out what was the matter.

Chapter 14

My 2 Big Inventions

AMERICA was now taking its place with
the rest of the world in the arts and sciences
and the year 1899 saw two great inventions,
by citizens of the United States, which were
universally hailed as revolutionary and daring. The first of these was the invention of
the straw, by Paul Whelton, a Boston news-

paper man. Mr. Whelton worked on the paper nights and in the daytime held a position as lifeguard at Revere Beach. In those days the Atlantic Ocean in the vicinity of Boston was way over your head and Revere bathers were being drowned by the thousands despite the courage and resourcefulness of Mr. Whelton and his two assistants, Nick Flatley and Mel Webb.

The chief lifeguard sat on the beach day after day, for months and months, watching the drowners drown and trying to figure out what was the matter. The idea came to him all of a heap.

"The idea came to me all of a heap," was the way he afterwards expressed it.

It occurred to him all of a heap that as each drowner was drowning for the third time, he seemed to appear to be clutching. And there was nothing to clutch at!

"If they just had something to clutch at!" thought Mr. Whelton, and that night, as he worked at the copy desk in the newspaper office, he thought suddenly of a straw, and the problem was solved.

Resigning from the paper, he started the quantity manufacture of straw and in a few days appeared on the beach with an arm-load of the new commodity. As each bather came out of the bath-house, Mr. Whelton approached him in a friendly way and said, smilingly: "Have a straw."*

People kept on drowning, but it was soon established that there was less danger if they bathed in straw stacks than in the ocean.

Mr. Whelton would not take money for the straws doled out for clutching purposes, but he soon found two other uses for his invention in which his conscience did not prevent acceptance of financial return. He began selling straws to the weather bureau and to sailors, outfielders and golfers, so they could tell which way the wind was blowing. And also, along about this time, the sport of camel hunting became quite popular through New England. "The ship of the desert" was very good eating as well

* Editor's note: Haverstraw, New Jersey, is said to have been named after Mr. Whelton.

as sufficiently foxy and elusive to make the pursuit interesting. New England camels, however, were deathly afraid of horses, horses, horses and you had to hunt them on foot.

And after you had walked miles and miles

New England camels were deathly afraid of horses, horses, horses and you had to hunt them on foot.

for a camel and finally caught up with him, there was no sure way of bringing him down. He scoffed at bullets, sniggered over knife thrusts and turned up his nose at lethal poisons. After endless experimenting by the wealthy nimrods of Beacon Street, Brookline and South Boston, it was found that a straw would reek havioc with his vertebrae, and Mr. Whelton's fortune was made.

The other invention of that year was the telephone. They are still trying to find the guy.

The first telephone exchange had only one number, Central 1. All the subscribers had to take that for their number and when you called up, there was no telling whom you would get.*

There was no rate by the month, each subscriber being charged a nickel per call. It made interesting gambling, dropping your nickel in the slot and then waiting to find out who would answer; if you expected, for example, to talk to, say, Flo Ziegfeld and a sweet voice at the other end of the line announced "This is Neysa McMein," or "This is Florence O'Denishawn," you had the same thrill as when a 50 to 1 shot which you have bet on at the track finishes first. Personally I always played in tough luck. I would call up Marilyn Miller and

* Editor's note: This is still true today.
Author's note: You spoke a full quart.

get Heywood Broun; or try for one of the Dolly Sisters and obtain Percy Hammond. It was an outrage.

The nickel a call system lasted until the repeal of the law preventing women from talking to one another. When women were at length permitted to call each other up, the company went into the hands of a telephone receiver because it was taking in only five cents a day.

In 1900, Robert Fulton invented and tried to introduce the automatic or dial telephone. His invention was turned down, unwillingly, by the phone trust in compliance with a petition from people in the then infantile motion picture industry, who argued that the strain of attempting to learn the alphabet would reek havioc with their Art.

Chapter 15

Sport Writer on *The Rabies*

In 1900 I turned over my medical practice to a bystander and went to work as
a sport writer on *The Rabies,* one of the
first of the so-called tabloid newspapers.
This was long before the tabloids became
so painfully reticent and dignified, and the
editors of the various departments were
annually selected from the graduating class
of the Oklahoma School of Oafs. The sporting editor under whom I worked was an
unrecognized cousin of Will Rogers named
Haney Thwack. He had been sent to the
school to be cured of a penchant for oatmeal and was given his diploma in spite of
the very obvious fact that the cure was
nowhere near complete. In fact, the first
day I reported at his desk, I found the same
covered with receptacles of all kinds filled
with the pompous cereal in different stages

of preparation. "Oatmeal Haney" was what the boys called him behind his back, and once or twice he overheard and just smiled. There was no offending "Oatmeal Haney."*

"Lardner," he said to me, "there's a coming golf champion down in Georgia named Bobby Jones. He is now a year old, or will be in a few years. I want you to get a picture of him in the bathtub and a good human nature, personality interview."

"But, Mr. Thwack," I remonstrated, "how can I get an interview with a man that age? Why, I don't suppose he can even talk plain."

"Age makes no difference with most Georgians," replied my superior, testing the cereal with his knee. "They hardly ever get so they can talk plain."

Bobby was splashing at a great rate when I was admitted to the lavatory.

"What are you doing, Mr. Jones?" was my first question.

* Editor's note: Unless you deprived him of the cereal.

Author's note: That is understood.

[85]

"Me take baff," he lisped. "Me no lika baff. Min's me of a watah hazard."

It was comical to hear him.*

"How are you getting along with your golf?" I asked.

"Ah is jes' tryin' to mastah the spoon," he said. "Dis mo'nin' at bretfus Ah used it fo' de fustes' time an'—an'—(he laughed at the memory) Ah spilt evahthing."

The youngster then posed for flashlights, with the stopper out, with the stopper in, with the tub full and with the tub empty. "Oatmeal Haney" congratulated me on my handling of the assignment and I was sent to interview Neysa McMein.

Miss McMein proved an interesting talker, once you could understand her dialect, as different from the Jones boy's as a couple of eighth notes.

I asked her where she had got the idea of drawing covers.

"Me getty idee from ol' Mis' Pukkins," she said. "Ol' Mis' Pukkins, she use' draw covers fo' de big hotel in Quincy, Illinois.

* Editor's note: Was it?

[86]

Soon as de gues' leave dere room in de mo'nin', she draw all de covers and let de beds air."

Miss McMein recounted the difficulties of her early career. I forget just what she

One of the rules provided that members of the sporting department get weighed every day before reporting for work.

did say. She overcame them some way or other and today her cover charge is $1500.00. The friendship begun at that time ripened into something grotesque and right now there is a saying along Broadway that wherever you find Neysa McMein, Ring Lardner is probably home working.

One of the rules in *The Rabies* office provided that members of the sporting department get weighed every day before reporting for work and if they weighed over 135 pounds stripped (as most of them usually were), they would have to go into some other department. This was in the days prior to Prohibition and I was drinking a great deal of water, with the result that one afternoon I tipped the beam at 141.*

"Oatmeal Haney" was loath to let me go and when I was ordered to report to the city editor, he made a scene, which he afterwards tried to sell to the Follies.

The city editor, Tom Bilgewater, regarded me at first wonderingly, then tenderly.

"Well," he said, when he had regained the use of his voice, "you are a very likely looking fellow."†

* Editor's note: There was also a rule against tipping the beam.

† Editor's note: Bilgewater was known among his intimates as "Blind" Bilgewater.

Author's note: You have him confused with some other Bilgewater. This Bilgewater was known as "Keen Eye" Bilgewater.

Wife's note: Dinner is ready.

Chapter 16

Star Reporter for *The Rabies*

OLD timers will have no difficulty in re-
calling the Helsh murder, and veteran newspaper men have never tired of compliment-
ing me on my work in connection therewith.
It was my first assignment as star reporter
for *The Rabies* and the fact that I was
chosen for the task speaks volumes for my
city editor, who was violently drunk at the
time.

For the benefit of half-witted readers, I
will recount the Helsh case in brief. Wallace
Helsh was a wealthy barn tearer in Pennsylvania. He went all over the state tearing
down barns so horses could get more air.
Mrs. Helsh was the former Minnie Blaggy,
prominent in Philadelphia society and the
daughter of Blotho Blaggy, who was in
charge of one of the switches in the Broad
Street railroad yards. Young Helsh and
Miss Blaggy became acquainted on one of

the former's barnstorming tours and were married two weeks after their first meeting. At the time of the murder, they had been married three years and Mrs. Helsh (née Blaggy) was expecting a baby, the child of one of her sisters. The baby was supposed to arrive on the 12:09 (midnight) train and the police first believed that the murder had grown out of a quarrel between the Helshes over which of them should sit up and meet it. This theory was based on the testimony of a neighbor, Basil Kidney, who said he had been hiding behind a book in the Helsh living room and overheard the following conversation:

"Will you sit up and meet our niece?" This from Mrs. Helsh.

"No." This from Helsh.

"Why not?"

"Because I don't water meter."

The witness did not hear any more of the conversation because it was then time for him to go on to another neighbor's house, the Quimbys, and hide in their living room. He was an habitual living room hider. But

half an hour after his departure from the
Helsh home, a mysterious voice called up
the police headquarters at Bryn Mawr and
announced that there had been a murder
at 24 Vine Street. This was not where the

A mysterious voice called up and announced that there had
been a murder at 24 Vine Street.

Helshes lived, which made it all the more
puzzling.

"Dig right into this!" said my city editor. "Comb Philadelphia, find out who did
it and get lots of pictures."

"How about my transportation?" I inquired.

"You can have carte blanche," was his
reply.

But thinking he referred to a dog cart and an old horse named Blanche, which conveyed our society reporter to and from her work every day, I declined his offer and went to Philadelphia by rail. My mistake was profitable, for the first man I met when I rolled from under the train at Broad Street was Blotho Blaggy, Mrs. Helsh's father.

"How about the murder, Mr. Blaggy?" I asked.

"Fine," he said. "They have arrested my little four-year-old grandchild, who was on her way to visit her aunt and uncle, but they can't pin anything on her. She hates pins; says she is too old for them."

Next morning, *The Rabies* made all the other tabloids look silly. Across the front page we had a streamer, "Child Murder Suspect Balks at Pins!" and under it were pictures of Lillian Gish, who had appeared on the screen at a Chestnut Street theatre that week, and of Chief Bender, making a balk. On Page 2 was my story of the murder and on Page 3, the first chapter of Mrs.

Helsh's diary, of which I have preserved a copy and will reprint a few paragraphs:

"Oo, Oo, diary, I am going to keep oo and write in oo every day and when I am a ole, ole lady bug, I will read oo and live over the days of my honeymoon.

"Daddy was a baddy, baddy boy today. I asked um to bwing me a ittsy bittsy diamond wing and he fordotted all about it and when I scolded um he swang for my jaw and knocked out some toofums that my real honest to goodness daddy had give me for a wedding pwesent.

"Oo never can tell what a red hot daddy will do-oo-oo."

I have perhaps forgotten to mention that when the police finally reached the Helsh home, Helsh was nowhere to be seen and Mrs. Helsh (née Blaggy) was playing a game of Bemis with her little niece. Asked when she expected her husband, she said the hour of his arrival always depended on the number and toughness of the barns he had visited, but he usually got back about six o'clock. The police then arrested the niece and left a guard to receive Helsh if and when he showed up. Sure enough, just at six o'clock he reached home and found dinner ready.

On the following morning, *The Rabies* printed pictures of Georges Carpentier, June Walker and Miss Omaha on the beach at Atlantic City and a portrait of the bath-tub in which Mrs. Helsh's sister had bathed her little girl before sending her on the fatal visit. I was given a bonus of $50 and spent it and the next two weeks waiting around for some more excitement.

Chapter 17

Promoted to Contest Editor

In the days of which I am now writing, Horace Greeley and Ben Hecht were joint editors of *The Rabies*. They edited all the news that came in about different joints around town. They received only a small salary, but were given a share of the paper's profits; therefore it was to their interest that the circulation and, consequently, the advertising be built up. One evening Mr. Greely called me into his private bath.*

As I entered he said, "Young man, go wash," and pointed to the bowl.†

When I had dried the both of us, Mr. Greeley said:

* Editor's note: Tabloid editors then worked in private baths instead of private offices.

† Editor's note: This remark of Mr. Greeley's has often been misquoted as "Young man, go west," and "Young man, go mah jongg," and sometimes even as "Young man, go get my slippers."

Author's note: Some of the misquotations have been laughable.

"Kid" (he called me kid), "the more people that buys this paper, the better for I and Ben. Now the best circulation getters is contests and we are going to make you

As I entered Mr. Greeley said, "Young man, go wash."

contest editor with carte blanche to offer whatever prizes you like in every kind of contest you can think of. Est-ce que c'est claire de lune?" ("Is it clear?")

I nodded my head and left him. On my way back to the city room, I encountered Charley Cautious, a fellow reporter.

"Whose private bath have you been in?" he inquired.

"Horace's," I replied.

"Horace's?" he repeated.

"Horace's," I said.*

After a rub-down, I went to work contriving contests. My first idea was an essay contest on "Why I Married Mr. Hopper," but it proved a failure ·as, at that time, there were only three persons eligible to the competition and two of the three would not, or could not, reply. The next one went over with a bang. It was a guessing contest of famous men. The names of the men, with a few of the letters left out, were printed in groups of five a day and prizes amounting to $50,000 were offered to those sending the most nearly correct answers, accompanied by a twelve thousand word article on boo scorpions.†

* Editor's note: This was probably the origin of the song, "Horace's, Horace's, Horace's."

† Editor's note: A boo scorpion was a sort of spider that went around booing ball players, actors and cock-eyed spaniels.

In the paper the first day we had "Abr-ham L-nc-ln; Th-mas Edis-n; Charl-s Ch-plin; Jac- B-rrymore; Charl-s D-ckens."

On the second day— "J-mes A. G-rfield; U. S. Gra-t; Robert E. L-e; M-rk Antony; H-rry K. Th-w."

And on the third day— "G-orge Ade; J-seph J-fferson; Irvin S. Co-b; H. L. M-ncken; J-hn P-ul J-nes."

Prior to the inauguration of this contest, *The Rabies* had a paid circulation of 126. To be eligible to compete, you had to sub-scribe to the paper for at least six months, and an even half million people entered the competition, raising our total circulation to 500,126.

Now comes the strange part of it. Of the half million articles on boo scorpions, every one seemed to be the work of a master of the subject; in fact, the articles were so uniformly convincing and scathingly de-nunciatory that Congress started a na-tion-wide campaign against these ribald vermin and succeeded in exterminating them. Today one speaks of a boo scorpion much the same as of a dinosaur or a mah jongg fiend.*

But it was unnecessary, not to say impossible, to award any of the prizes, because none of the 500,000 competitors came anywhere near guessing the names of the famous men. Almost without exception the answers sent in were Abraham Lincoln, Thomas Edison, Charles Chaplin, Jack Barrymore, Charles Dickens, James A. Garfield, U. S. Grant, Robert E. Lee, Mark Antony, Harry K. Thaw, George Ade, Joseph Jefferson, Irvin S. Cobb, H. L. Mencken and John Paul Jones. Whereas the correct answers were—Abroham Luncalm, Thamas Edisun, Charlus Choplin, Jace Burrymore, Charlas Duckens, etc., every one of them a real person, known to me by hearsay and each famous in the locality in which he lived. For example, the

* Editor's note: The author was probably not aware of the fact that the last named pixy is still running amuck in many places, notably East Hampton, Long Island, in spite of the vigilance of the narcotic squad.

tenth one, guessed by all the competitors as Harry K. Thaw, was in reality a man named Hurry K. Thew, a well known Kansas City bossop tamperer, who drove half the K. C. housewives crazy by sneaking through their gardens by night, tampering with their bossops.

This contest virtually made *The Rabies* and nearly wrecked me. For months afterwards I lay in a hospital, at death's door from the strain I had gone through.

Dr. Pine explained that Dr. Gasp had been drinking heavenly.

Chapter 18

Hallowe'en in Polyandry Hospital

ARRANGEMENTS were made by the proprietors of *The Rabies* to have me examined by two of the most eminent diagnosticians then in New York, Dr. Pine and Dr. Gasp. Dr. Gasp had 104 degrees, while his partner's temperature was normal. Dr. Pine explained that Dr. Gasp had been drinking heavenly.*

* Editor's note: The author evidently means "heavily."

Author's note: The editor is evidently a f—l.

The two doctors made me strip to my nightgown and went all over me with a horoscope. Their diagnosis was chronic alfalfa and they said I must be rushed to a hospital and tattooed.

On the third day of October, 1896, I was ridden on a rail to the Polyandry Hospital and taken in charge by Dr. Barnacle, who immediately put me under the ether. The janitor found me there two days later and lifted me onto a bed. That night I was removed to the operating room and tattooed in three places. On my right knee they did a picture of Whiteman's band playing before the Chesapeake and Ohio station agent at Clifton Forge; on my chest, the first Battle of the Marne, and on my (at that time) rather high forehead, the piano score of Parsifal.

Operations in those days were quite painful as the anæsthetics employed were not nearly so effective as those now in use. In my case, and all other major surgical operations such as appendicitis, internal ulsters, etc., the patient was allowed to suck a lemon; it was not until 1899 that they gave you an aspirin tablet in cases of the removal of a leg or an arm.*

I recovered so wonderfully that after the

The janitor found me there two days later.

third day Dr. Barnacle ceased his daily visits to me and left me in the care of the internes (so called because every time you wanted one of them, he had just turned in). My room, which I shared with the Marx

* Illinois: 491; Shields v. Shields.

brothers, the Dolly sisters and the Fairbanks twins, was a veritable paunch of flowers and I received so many telegrams that the company sent them in separate envelopes.

On the thirtieth of the month I was pronounced cured and told I could go home, but the nurses, who had taken quite a fancy to me, persuaded me to remain and participate in the Hallowe'en pranks, which were then a feature of hospital life.*

Well, the things we didn't do would be easier to tell than the things we did.†

Among the pranks I recall particularly are the following:

1. The patient in Room 18 had been almost fatally burned in an apartment house fire. A crowd of twenty other patients and nurses gathered outside his door and yelled "Fire!" till he jumped out the window.

* Editor's note: And still are.
Author's note: I didn't know that.
† Editor's note: Then why not tell the things you didn't do?
Author's note: Why not shut up?

As Room 18 was on the fifth floor, you can imagine his surprise.

2. In Room 4 was a man who had fallen out of a rug and broken three ribs. We sent him spare-ribs for his supper.

3. Room 6A was occupied by a ball player with Charley horse. We sent him some oats.

4. I have forgotten what ailed the woman in Room 11 and what we did to her.

Those are just a few of the pranks we played in Polyandry Hospital on Hallowe'en, 1896.

Chapter 19

A Soft Job

DR. PEARSON, on the day of my release from the hospital, warned me that I would have to be careful for at least a year and advised me not to return to the nerve wracking profession of journalism.

"Get into some calmer line of work," he said, "something that won't be much of a physical or mental strain."

"What, for instance, Duck?"* I inquired.

"The calmest, most leisurely calling I can think of," replied the doctor, "is that of a ticket agent in a large railroad terminal."

In compliance with this hint, I investigated and found that applicants for such a position were required to take a week's

---

*Editor's note: The author doubtless meant to say "Doc."

Author's note: The author meant what he said. Pearson was a notorious quack.

training. The training outfit consisted of a
ticket rack in which were tickets to every
town in the country, arranged in alpha-
betical order; a flat shelf equipped with date
stamps, pencils and pens, and an iron grating which separated the student from the
practice customers.

The applicant had to report at 8 o'clock
in the morning. His first duty was to break
the points of the pens and pencils and set
the date stamp either six months behind or
ahead of the current date. Then, all day
long until 6 in the evening, crowds of practice customers kept coming up and standing
in front of the grating. The applicant was
instructed to keep his eyes fixed firmly on
the floor except twice during the day,
when he might look at a customer and wait
on him, there being a rule that no one
agent might sell more than two tickets per
diem.

The first practice customer whom the
applicant deigned to notice would, we will
say, ask for a ticket to Baltimore. The applicant would look through the T's, M's, K's

and any other six letters; then turn his attention to the B part of the rack and produce a ticket to Baltimore. He would then twirl his date stamp six months ahead or behind as the case might be, and stamp the ticket. If the fare to Baltimore was $4.10, he would have to borrow a good pencil or pen from another applicant and write one under the other, the figures $4.00 and .10, on an envelope; then scratch his head and add them and write down the total—$4.10. The practice customer would then submit a five dollar bill and the applicant would repeat to himself the names of all his friends in a painstaking effort to think of somebody who might have change.

I learned all these tricks easily and was given a position at one of the windows in Grand Central Station, New York. On the first day I lived up to the rules, looked at only two people and sold two tickets. But after that, my natural imaginativeness and individuality overcame my sense of duty and I proceeded to revolutionize the ticket selling industry. One or two samples of my methods, and their results, may prove interesting.

A beautiful widow with two children

A beautiful widow with two children.

asked for tickets to Peekskill.

"Madam," I said, "Peekskill has many attractions, but I think you would find Ardsley just as nice, and it's nearer and cheaper."

"All right, make it Ardsley," said she.

[109]

"And how about my kiddies? Are they half fare?"

"Not half as fair as their mummy," said I. "But joking to one side, I think it is a mistake to take them at all. I know a fellow in Ardsley who wants to marry a widow and I will gladly give you a letter of introduction to him. But he hates children and if you were to show up with those two, well, to put it mildly, whelps, your chances of matrimony would go glimmering."

"Mamma," whined one of the whelps, "let's go glimmering."

This remark may have settled the issue; at any rate, the little lady made the trip alone, leaving her children in the waiting room, where, I heard later, they were quite a nuisance for a couple of days; after which they disappeared. Their mother married the Ardsley wight, who left her, in four years, with three new children, or one up on what she had before, to say nothing of the superior quality of the later litter.

On another occasion, my frankness led me into a lasting comradeship with Nora

Bayes, who came to my window one afternoon and demanded a ticket to Albany and a lower berth to Syracuse.

"But, Miss Bayes," I remonstrated, "if you are only going to Albany, why do you want a berth to Syracuse?"

"Because I always sleep past my station," was her reply.

This struck me as so comical that I hurried up to the athletic field of the University of Columbia and watched some of the men practice broad jumping.

Chapter 20

Dan Boone's Joke

ONE of the traits or characteristics for which the writer has been noted in recent years is dignity, self-possession. Only the other day I was complimented on this by no less a personage than Mr. Charles M. Schwab.

"Lardy," he said in his enchanting southern drawl, "you certainly have a lot of poise."

"Yes," I replied lightly. "Three are at home and one is away at school."

But at the time of which I am now writing, I was so playful and "flighty" that it had never occurred to me to enter a vocation where solemnity and composure were deemed essential and it was a shock to me when my good friend Daniel Boone suggested that I go into politics.

"Lardy," he said, "why don't you run for an office?"

"Why? Do you think it is going to rain?" was my laughing retort.

Boone resented my levity and never spoke to me again, and every night for several months thereafter, he attempted to "get

Boone attempted to "get even" by ringing my front door bell, then hiding behind some bushes in the yard.

even" by ringing my front doorbell, then hiding behind some bushes in the yard and shouting "Pretty fellow!" when I came to the door. It is my firm belief that if I had taken his suggestion seriously that day, he would, by the tremendous force of his personality, have pushed me into a judge-ship or at least got me on a jury. As it

was, through reading "The Americaniza-
tion of Edward Bok," I became interested
in the collection of autographs and found it,
for a time, the most engrossing sport in
which I had ever participated.

In emulation of Mr. Bok, I started right
after the "big fellows," my first "objective"
being Senator Smoot. A servant informed
me that the Senator was taking a bath.
Luckily (for me) he had neglected to lock
the bathroom door, so when I walked in on
him, took all the towels and told him firmly
that he could not have one until he had
signed my autograph album, there was
nothing for him to do but comply. He was
greatly amused at what he termed my
bonhomie.

My next quarry was Madame Modjeska
whose signature I obtained by tickling her
feet with a sprig of holly until she was glad
to do anything to get rid of me. By similar
pranks and pleasantries I landed all the
Presidents. I became known as a kind of a
pest, but just the same I am the owner today of the greatest collection of famous

autographs in the world and the only question is what to do with it.

It was for the purpose of adding to this collection that I visited Philadelphia in September of 1926; notables from all over the country were there at the time to witness the great heavyweight championship prize-fight between Jack Dempsey and Gene Tunney, but it developed that very few of them could write their names. The fight went ten rounds and the judges gave the decision to Mr. Tunney and a lot of us boys thought it would have been a horse on Mr. Dempsey if they hadn't. It was reported after the fight that the winner was considering an offer from C. C. Pyle to join the ranks of the professionals.

This was my first trip to the City of Brotherly Love* since Gen. Smedley Butler was sent there to clean it up. The result of his work was a revelation. Unless you had brought your own liquor, you could no longer get a drink in Philadelphia without asking for it.

* Editor's note: Philadelphia.

[115]

Philadelphia at that time had a boxing commission something like New York's (No offense meant). The commission, which was appointed by the Governor, named the judges that decided the outcome of fights. On this occasion Gov. Pinchot said he would like to see Mr. Tunney win and it may have been to save the commission and its judges from embarrassment that Mr. Dempsey acted as if the whole party was a big surprise to him. He seemed to have at last mastered the boxing style of Farmer Lodge who helped him prepare for his fight with Firpo some years before.

A man sitting right back of me kept insisting that Mr. Dempsey ought to be disqualified for violating Pennsylvania's boxing code, which barred the rabbit punch. I was not familiar with the rules, but Jack certainly punched like a rabbit.

Chapter 21

I First Marry in Central Park—
Lapland Lady for Bride

WE now come to my first marriage. The girl was a born Laplander and landed in my lap during the course of a quiet week-end party at the Curley estate on Long Island. I suppose I was fascinated by the music of her broken English as much as by the blonde perfection of her 212 pounds of bubbling youth.

"Listen, hon'," were her first words: "Ise mahty thusty. Is you-all goin' to fetch me some mo' dat dere gin?"

As she Lapped the fresh made spirits, I made her tell me of herself. Her name was Hugga—Hugga Much—and she was the daughter of an Eskimo society woman who had fallen in love with her family's Lap dog trainer.

"Mah mammy was sho 'nough 'folks'" she said proudly.

When the party was over and I had gone back to New York, she obtained my address and began showering me with mash notes,

"Listen, hon'," were her first words: "Is you-all goin' to fetch me some mo' dat dere gin?"

written in the same stertorous drawl. She was the most persistent of all the women who have ever marked me as their goal and it soon became evident that fighting her off was a waste of time. I finally said yes, and

[118]

the scene that followed defies description. Dignified men marched the streets ringing cowbells and fairly reeking with confetti; women tore each other's clothes, and even little children asked, "Where is nurse?" and "What is all the hullabaloo?"

Now followed preparations for the wedding. I was for having some of my friends as ushers and got as far as selecting Robert Benchley and Robert Sherwood, two beggars of *Life*, but Hugga, always strong for system and efficiency, insisted on my engaging the ushers from Madison Square Garden. I wanted the ceremony held at Old Trinity; Hugga said it was below her station—she usually got off at Columbus Circle. So we decided to put it on in Central Park, which was convenient for both of us and big enough to accommodate most of our buddies.*

My best man was Paul Whelton of the Boston Wheltons. He was then employed at Sing Sing prison as an electric chair

* Editor's note: "Buddies" is not in any dictionary and may be a colloquialism meaning, perhaps, clowns or funny men.

[119]

tester, his duties being to sit in the chair just before an execution and inform the electrician regarding the current, whether it was just right or too strong or not strong enough. "Volts" Whelton, his buddies* called him.

Hugga's bridesmaid was Texas Guinan and her maid of honor was Elizabeth Barrett (Peaches) Browning.†

It rained the night before the wedding, but the park had been covered with tarpaulin and when this had been removed, Judge Landis examined the turf and ruled

* Editor's note: There is that word again.

† Author's note: At this point I wish to correct an error that was made by the New York newspapers in their account of the wedding. I was repeatedly referred to as the groom, though I have had nothing to do with the care of a horse since I was twelve years old, and then only as a favor. The mistake probably was due to a misunderstanding by an Associated Press reporter, who, when my engagement was announced, called up Hugga's mother, Sitta Much, and asked if she was satisfied with me as a son-in-law. Mrs. Much replied: "I certainly am. He is a hustler." The reporter, no doubt, thought

that the ceremony must go on. Hugga was greeted with commingled boos and cheers. She seemed perfectly calm. I learned afterward that this was the sixth time she had

I entered leaning on the arm of a taxi driver.

tempted Hymen. Mayor Walker of New

she said "hostler." The two words "hostler" and "hustler" sound a great deal alike, especially in Eskimo.*

* Editor's note: Another amusing incident is told concerning that same telephone conversation. When the reporter first got the bride's mother on the wire, he said: "Mrs. Much?" and she replied: "Yes. A great deal."

[121]

York and Dudley Field Malone presented her with the keys to Key West and McKeesport and everybody stood up and bared their chests while the band played the Lapland national anthem.*

Nick Altrook and Al Schacht next put on their comical burlesque channel swim and then I entered leaning on the arm of a taxi driver. It was all he could do to hold me up.†

The one ring service was read by an official of the Lotus club and we adjourned to the wedding breakfast, consisting of half a grapefruit, cereal, choice of bacon or ham and eggs, or country sausage and wheat cakes, toast, rolls or muffins, coffee, tea, milk, cocoa, Kaffee Hag, open 7 to 9:30. Sundays, 7:30 to 10.

* Editor's note: A custom. The anthem referred to begins, "Lap and the world laps with you."
† Driver's note: I never held nobody up.

"And when is it going to open?" she asked.

Chapter 22

On My Honeymoon

AFTER the wedding breakfast, my first act was to get a shave and a shine. Then I sought out my bride and broached her on the subject of a honeymoon.

"Where would you like to go on your honeymoon?" I broached her.

"I don't care," she rebroached, "as long as it is a place where we can be by ourselves."

So I hailed a taxi and we caught the eleven o'clock express for Philadelphia and visited the Sesquicentennial Exposition. Hugga remarked that it reminded her of her native town, Skulk, in Lapland.*

We strolled up and down the Gladway and she asked me why it was so named. I replied that it was named in honor of the people who had backed the Exposition.

"And when is it going to open?" she asked.

"Who?" I rejoined.

"The Exposition," said Hugga.

"It opened early last summer," I told her.

"Oh!" said Hugga.

She was always making mistakes, but was always quick to acknowledge them.

I showed her the huge stadium in which Jack Dempsey had lost his title and I my shirt. I pointed out the spot where the ring had been located and the spot, six feet away from it, where I had sat. She was amazed when I informed her that the "house" had

* Author's note: Skulk is not really a town at all; merely a fishing smack.

been sold out that night and exclaimed at the vast distance between the scene of battle and the most remote seats.

"Why, the people in some of those seats," she said, "couldn't really tell whether it was a fight or a schottische!"

"Neither could I," I replied, laughingly.

Hugga had brought me a dowry of $3,500 and as we both preferred small towns to large, we decided to invest in some business in a desirable residential community up-state from New York. Through a friend of Hugga's father we learned that the post office in a place called Gluten was for sale. Gluten had a population of nearly two thousand, of whom more than eight hundred were dogs.

"It's a great little town!" said Hugga's father's friend. "It's got running water and two spigots."

Hugga was quite practical.

"Don't let's be carried away by blurbs," she said. "It seems to me that the post office in a town where the inhabitants are forty per cent dogs is not likely to be very profitable. Dogs, or at least the dogs I have known (she flushed) are not great letter writers."

"But the dogs of Gluten are male dogs," retorted her father's friend.*

"Of course," put in my father-in-law, Mr. Much, "you can't expect big profits from a small town post office if you run it solely as a post office. The idea is to sell stamps, post cards, envelopes, etc., only when necessary and depend on other kinds of merchandise for your main source of revenue."

"And the town being what it is, I would advise you to carry a large line of canine accessories," added his friend.†

Thus it was that my young wife and I

* Author's note: His name, we found out afterwards, was Webster.

Editor's note: There was a family of Websters in Elmira.

Author's note: This was a different Webster.

Editor's note: The same spelling.

† Editor's note: Presumably Webster.

Author's note: Not related to the Elmira Websters.

began a mercantile career which netted us over a thousand dollars the first year and attracted the attention of the then Postmaster General, Basil Paunch. On our front window was inscribed a small sign, "United States Post Office," and under it, a much larger sign, "Everything for the Dog." It was a simple matter to divert customers from their original intention of purchasing stamps and persuade them to buy something doggy, at a much greater profit to us. One example of our method will suffice. On our first day, a Mrs. Femur came in and asked for a two-cent stamp.

"You don't want a stamp," said Hugga. "What you need is a muzzle."

"Perhaps you are right," said Mrs. Femur, and before she had left the place we had sold her a $12.00 amber muzzle which netted us $10.45.

Another of our big winners, which we usually sold in place of post cards, was fleabane concocted by Hugga herself out of drippings from Queen Marie's diary.

[127]

Chapter 23

My Romance Blasted

THIS chapter is one I would not have written but for the insistence of my relatives and friends who are aware of the injustice done me by the press and have persuaded me that it is only fair to myself and them that I state, for once and all, the true facts of the case.

The subject is my divorce from my first wife, Hugga Much, or rather (thanks to perjured evidence and a "judge" so crooked that the state automobile association had fairly plastered his body with signs reading "Danger! Reverse Curve Ahead!") her divorce from me.

We had been married only a few years when the storm broke. We were living in Gluten, N. Y., and while nominally proprietors of the post office there, were cleaning up a tidy fortune through the barter of dog muzzles, assorted leashes and fleabane. It netted us so little profit to conduct the regular business of a post office that we had discouraged Glutenites from buying such things as envelopes and stamps, telling them either that we were just out of those

At first sight of Hugga he forgot all about the business that
had brought him.

commodities or that the ones we had in stock were infected, or otherwise damaged.

This finally, through some jealous busy-body, was called to the attention of Post-master General Basil Paunch and that official personally came up from Washington to investigate. At his first sight of Hugga, he forgot all about the business that had brought him and fell violently in love. His love was returned and one day I stumbled upon the ungainly pair playing "Nine Men's Morris" at the municipal filling station. To avoid a scene, I ordered Paunch to visit me at my office and when I met him there, we had quite a talk.

He told me it got awfully hot in Washington in the summer months, but the springs and falls were lovely and the winters much milder than in New York. The principal streets, he said, were named after states or letters of the alphabet.*

I started my divorce suit in Sullivan County, but my wife asked for a change of venue as the doctor said it would do her

---

* Editor's note: My sister Cora, who visited Washington at the time of President McKinley's inauguration, wrote me that G street was one of the main business thoroughfares.

Author's note: It was, and still is.

Editor's note: It was during this trip that Cora became acquainted with Wayne Pardee.

Author's note: Not *the* Wayne Pardee!

Editor's note: A nephew.

good. Neither of us had ever been to Chicago for a really long stay, so we chose the Crescent City for the scene of action. We found it much the same as New York except that the citizens carried muskets instead of canes. State Street had just been provided with a blazing new system of lights as a result of complaints of machine gunners that because of poor visibility, hundreds of harmless matricides had been mistaken for bystanders and shot down or up.

On the day preceding the opening of the case, forty-six special trainloads of co-respondents reached the city. In the forenoon they were received by the then Mayor, Gifford Pelk, and given the keys to their trunks, which had been opened by mistake. A tour of the Stockyards and breweries took up the balance of the day, and then came the problem of sleeping accommodations. Even with cots lining all the halls, the hotels were unable to take care of the co-respondents named either by Hugga or me and a panic was averted only by a great idea born in the brain of a well-known newspaper man, James Crusinberry.

"First," he said, "get everybody to bed that has a bed. Then assemble the left-overs and tell them to take a walk around the block. Thus they will all be provided with a lodging."

"Where?" inquired a man with a pointed beard.

"In the Morgue," replied Mr. Crusinberry.

"One time," put in another stranger, "we had a case somewhat similar to this in my home town, Cincinnati. There were so many co-respondents that the hotels could not accommodate half of them. So a committee of citizens went to the outskirts of town and put up tents for the overflow. They called it the Tent City."

"That wouldn't do here," said a man whose name turned out to be Frank Bering.

"Why not?" asked the stranger.

"Because," said Mr. Bering, "Chicago is the Second City, not the Tent."

Chapter 24

My Divorce Trial

THE day of my divorce hearing dawned bright and clear. By the time court opened, it was just right for the spectators, but a little warm for the litigants. The vast crowd was on hand early and appeared highly entertained at the antics of the rival bands. The twelve thousand co-respondents named by me made a tremendous hit when they marched into the court-room, stopped and formed a C and pointing at my wife, sang their alma mater, "Yes Sir," That's! My Baby!

Hugga and I were called to the centre of the room, where we first shook hands and then cut for positions. Hugga cut the high card and chose to sit near the west window, where there was a slight breeze. The officials were Judge Ogle, Attorney Dumb for me, the plaintiff, and Attorney Wheedle for Hugga, the defendant.*

*Editor's note: According to newspaper accounts, Mr. Lardner turned down a suggestion of his coun-

A transcript of the testimony will best show what a raw deal I got. The only witness was Clena Sheets, a chambermaid in the Baldwin Hotel at Curve, Tenn.

Direct examination by Attorney Dumb:

Q. Did you ever see this defendant? *A.* Yes.

Q. Where? *A.* Who?

Q. This defendant. *A.* I seen her at the Baldwin Hotel, in Curve.

Q. Who? *A.* This defendant.

Q. Was she alone? *A.* Why, I suppose so. I don't think they ever was a time when we had more than one guest.

Q. Did you know she was married? *A.* I know she wasn't. She had a single room.

Q. What was the number of her room? *A.* 502.

Cross examination by Attorney Wheedle:

Q. Miss Sheets, how is it that you remember the number of this defendant's

sel's that the case be tried before a petty jury, saying that if Hugga found out they were the least bit petty, she would insist on a party instead of a trial.

room? *A.* I remember it because it's the only room in the hotel.

Q. If there is only one room, in the hotel, why is it numbered 502? *A.* That's his favorite number.

Q. Who? *A.* Jack Downey, who runs the hotel.

Re-direct examination by Attorney Dumb:

Q. Miss Sheets, you are under oath and you will find it to your advantage to tell the truth. Kindly give the honest reason why the only room in your hotel is numbered 502. *A.* All the other rooms were burned up in the big fire.

Q. Leaving only Room 502 standing? *A.* That's right.

Q. Was Room 502 on the fifth floor? *A.* Where and the he—ll do you think it would be? (Laughter.)

A. And were the office floor and the mezzanine and all the rooms below, above and on the same floor as 502 destroyed by the fire? *A.* Yes. (Catcalls.)

Q. And Room 502 alone was unscathed.

[135]

How do you account for that? *A*. I have nothing to do with the accounting. That is attended to by the bookkeeper. (Bird calls and bugle calls.)

Q. Was this defendant in Room 502 at the time of the fire? *A*. Yes.

Q. How do you know? *A*. If she wasn't, she'd of been burned. (Violins, violoncellos, etc., pizzicato.)

Q. Have you ever seen any of these co-respondents? *A*. Yes, all of them.

Q. Where? *A*. In the writing room of the hotel.

Q. What were they doing? *A*. Co-re-sponding. (Cries of "Goodness!" and "Touchdown! Touchdown!")

Judge Ogle: "It seems to me that this defendant proved herself a woman of extraordinary acumen in selecting the only fireproof room in the hotel. If she had used half as sound judgment in choosing a husband, the less said about it the better. The court finds for the defendant, awards her $12.00 per week alimony, a Colonial house within walking distance of a golf course, half a mile from the railroad station, five master bedrooms, three baths, four servants' rooms with bath, three-car garage, electricity, water and gas, and might add that if she has no engagement for this evening, why neither has the court."

Thus ended my first marital venture and I will state here that I bear no ill will toward Hugga, who, I am told, is doing very well as an elevator starter at the Olympic Games.

"The court might add that if she has no engagement for this evening, why neither has the court."

Chapter 25

Even Judge Ogle Smiled

In recounting the trial I forgot to include a couple of examples of the sparkling repartee between counsel for the opposing sides, which, I believe, are well worth publication. At one stage of the proceedings, my lawyer, Attorney Dumb, made the remark that Hugga's lawyer, Mr. Wheedle, looked as if he had forgotten to shave that morning.

"So do you!" replied Attorney Wheedle without an instant's hesitation.

"I'll bet your wife wishes she was single," said Attorney Dumb.

"Yours is!" retorted his opponent.

Not long after this tour de force Mr. Wheedle objected to Mr. Dumb's habit (amounting almost to a knack) of snapping the various court attendants' suspenders. It really was annoying, both to the attendants and the rest of us; the noise was deafening.*

* Editor's note: Consult William Holabird on "What Shall We Do With Suspender Snappers?'

"If the court pleases," said Mr. Wheedle, "I believe this trial could be gotten through with a great deal more pleasantly if counsel for the plaintiff would pay less attention to the attendants' suspenders."

"I presume counsel for the defense wears a belt," retorted Mr. Dumb sarcastically.

"I would like to belt you in the jaw!" exclaimed Mr. Wheedle.

"You look like a horse!" said Mr. Dumb.

"Is that why you keep riding me?" asked Mr. Wheedle.

Even Judge Ogle could not suppress a smile, but quickly recovered his dignity and pounded on his desk with dental floss.

This badinage probably had no effect on the outcome of the trial, but as a result of it, the two attorneys were later persuaded to give up the profession of law and join the staff of the *Harvard Lampoon*.

Like Jack Dempsey, I became popular in defeat and when I returned to New York I found awaiting me an invitation to attend an exclusive luncheon at the Plaza in honor of the Queen of Roumania. Those excluded were the assistant bell captain and Joe Muriosi of the men's washroom.

I found Marie a woman of a ready quick wit, a woman who spoke Roumanian with only a trace of accent. She was plainly dressed in a Mother Hubbard and Plus Fours.

"Po'k chops; dat's ma dish," she said to the waiter. "Bring me some o' dem po'k chops and sweet potato. An' make de po'k chops nice an' brown. Nice, brown po'k chops is somethin' Marie don't like nothin' else but."

"The watermelon is good today," suggested the waiter.

"Oh, dat watahmelon! Oh, dat watahmelyon hangin' on de vine!" sang her majesty, beating time with an oyster opener.

After dessert, the head porter introduced Col. William Grenfall, who helps open taxi doors at the Fifty-eighth Street entrance.

"Friends," said Col. Grenfall, "it is a

coincidence that royalty should visit America in this year of all years, the year of the Sesquicentennial Exposition as well as the hundredth anniversary of the *Youth's Companion*. This reminds me of a story told me last night by my good friend Junius Gab-

"Oh, dat watahmelyon hangin' on de vine!" sang her majesty, beating time with an oyster opener.

bett who calls trains at the Grand Central Station."

"What does he call them?" interrupted the Queen.

"Trains," replied Col. Grenfall with an amused smile. "You will stop me, I trust, if you have heard the story before. It seems there were——"

Col. Grenfall was paged at this point; it

developed there was a taxi at the Fifty-eighth Street entrance and the door stuck.*

The Queen, responding, said the only disturbing feature of her trip had been the announcement of the athletic break between Harvard and Princeton, which had apparently plunged the entire country in gloom and which she called the most important event in United States history since Marc Connelly, playing alone at Coldstream, missed a putt that would have given him a 124.

* Editor's note: Probably something the matter with it.

Author's note: Must have been.

Chapter 26

I Revolutionize Theatre Business

My memoirs are now drawing to a close. (Cries of "Touchdown! Touchdown!" and "We want Borah!") But it would be little less than criminal were I to complete the story of my life without explaining why I selected Great Neck, Long's Island, as the place to end my days. My second wife, a tall, gangling Swiss girl named Emma Geezle, whose father had made his money in Alpine stock, said she had lived all her life in a little haunch at the corner of Broadway and Forty-second street and she was sick of the bright lights.

"Take me," she said, "to some town where we won't be dazzled by the lights."

So I asked a prominent realtor to recommend a town where there would be no danger of being blinded by electricity.

"Great Neck," was his reply. "You will

find that some of the people out there get lit up quite often, but the houses hardly ever. If the weather report reads 'Cloudy,' or 'Light southwest winds,' the current becomes so affected that many a wife, attempting to dress for a party, has found herself frantically trying to complete her accouterment by donning a wing collar and a dinner jacket."

So Emma and I bought ourselves a love nook in Great Neck, christened it "The House of a Dozen Candles" and are now devoting most of our time to keeping the house in order, no small task when your menage consists of five servants, six children, four rooms and bath, a police dog, three mechanics and a full-grown leopard.

In my spare moments I devised a scheme which for a time revolutionized the musical comedy business in New York. In those days it was customary for producers of revues and other musical plays to seek to attract patronage by having their performers wear hardly any costumes.

The tights worn by chorus girls in old

time burlesque shows came to be regarded as too cumbersome and various committees on public morals were at their wits' ends for methods to compel the theater men to

It was really surprising to note the number of citizens who refused to undress before handing their seat checks to the ushers.

observe what they called the elements of decorum and attire their dancers and cory-phees in something more tangible than a square inch of gauze.

It was Mayor Walker who called me in to make suggestions. After a day's thought I concocted the following plan: To make it compulsory for all members of the audience to disrobe utterly before entering the theater.

At first, the Mayor could not see that this would make matters any better, but I quickly convinced him. As soon as the ordinance was passed, attendance at shows fell off so lamentably that most of the productions were obliged to close. It was really surprising, even to me, to note the number of citizens who refused to undress before presenting their seat checks to the ushers. Most of them complained that the play houses were too drafty.

At any rate, the producing managers' association soon petitioned the Mayor to have the ordinance wiped off the books and a compromise was readily effected whereby the audiences were permitted to remain clothed again provided the actors did likewise.

A banquet was given with me as the guest of honor and David Belasco, often referred to as the Master because he occupies the

Master's bedroom at the Belasco home, presented me with a lock of his hair.

In the concluding chapter I will tell of my declining years in Great Neck and the accident that resulted in my death.

Chapter 27

A Post-Mortem Message

BEFORE recounting the accident, it will be necessary to describe the locale of our Great Neck home and to name and picture a few of our then neighbors. As is perhaps known to a few of my less dumb readers, Great Neck is something of a literary and theatrical center.

Not far from us, on Cow Lane, lived Ed Streeter, author of the "Dere Mable" letters, for which I received many congratulations. In "the Estates" resided Sam Hellman, writer of short stories and inventor of the popular dessert, "Rind Wine," consisting of watermelon soaked in champagne.

Up the hill was the home of Gene Buck boasting a living room of such dimensions that fifty or one hundred guests often visited the Bucks in a single evening, each thinking he was the only one that had come.

Mr. Buck had formerly lived in a hovel of sixteen rooms, but when the first baby came, decided it was necessary to branch out. A second little Buck has since been added to the family and Gene is negotiating for the purchase or rental of the Paramount Building.

Our next door neighbors in the summer time were the H. B. Swopes. H. B. (Silent) Swope was the executive editor of The New York *World*. He and his madam had Company every week-end, Company being used in the military sense, full strength.

It got noised about that Emma and I had chow every Sunday about one o'clock and three or four platoons of our neighbors' Company, having gone breakfastless owing to the sleeping prowess of mine host and hostess, acquired the quaint habit of dropping in at our haunch at about that hour and making complimentary remarks about our children. When this ruse had been seen through at the expense of several fragments of chicken and cups of coffee, Emma stamped out the practice by posting a sign which read, "Try Our Table d'hôte $3.00."

In other parts of our village lived Bobby North, of the original Floradora Sextette; Ed Wynn, female impersonator; Raymond Hitchcock, soft shoe hoofer; Joe Santley, trap and drums; Arthur Hopkins, eccentric dancer; Sam Harris, the bridge authority; Ernest Truex, the Welsh comic; Oscar Shaw, gigolo; Frank Craven, the Tattooed Man; Bob Woolsey, proprietor of the Flea Circus; Tad Dorgan, designer of farm implements, and Thomas Meighan, "Is It a Man or Wolf?"

To say nothing of one of the Marx Brothers, who had recently bought a house, and Eddie Cantor, who had done the same and it was said that neither of them had come anywhere near paying cash.

It was doubtless as a result of this environment that the thing happened to me. I got up one morning and after my customary plunge down the staircase, I took my finger exercises, consisting of pointing first one finger and then the other at my wife. She made the remark that it would be a nice day to go out in the bay and fish for hake.*

Getting into my rowboat, I put on a No. 2 bait, a combination of a cockroach and the kind of salad they serve you in hospitals. I thought perhaps a hake would eat it, as nobody else would. I had hardly made my first cast when——†

* Editor's note: There has always been fine hake fishing in the bay on which the Lardner home fronts.

Author's note: Nobody ever caught a hake there yet.

Editor's note: Makes the chance of catching one all the better.

† Editor's note: At this point the author's memoirs are abruptly terminated. The coroner's jury brought in a verdict of "death by being hit in the stomach by a hake."

Author's note: Or death from stomach hake.

Getting into my rowboat I put on a number two bait.